Reviews of D

"What Lisa has in abundance
attitude and energy. It shapes her outlook on life and the
decisions she makes during her journey!

An easy read and relevant to all ages. It is fascinating,
stimulating, and inspirational. A highly recommended
read."

~ Vilde Aakeroy, Norway

"An inspirational read and following your heart always
worked for you. Sometimes we just know where our happy
place is and that's where we should be."

~ Moira McGregor, UK

"My takeaway from reading this book about Lisa's
experiences of life and death, joy and sorrow, is to "Live my
life on my terms, creating my own happiness" as I continue
to dream!"

~ Zing Nafzinger, USA

"You describe perfectly the sensations, feelings and fears
that you feel not living in your home country."

~ Coraline Lefebvre, Dubai

"It's a fantastic book, and I can't wait to hear about the
second part of her exciting life journey."

~ Rebecca Ronane, Provence, France

"Lisa's descriptive way of story-telling painted a really detailed picture of so many times in her life, and in so many places too. A fantastic read."

~ Jacqueline Kent, UK

"Lisa proves that determination and hard work can help you achieve your dreams. If you like reading about people and how they follow their dreams, as well as dealing with life's challenges, then this book is definitely one to read and be inspired by."

~ Tanya Clarke, UK

"An easy, good read of a true story with helpful tips if you are thinking of moving to France or settling down there."

~ Danni Fraser, UK

"Even though our career paths and lifestyle were very different, Lisa's drive and determination to never give up on her dreams really resonated with me."

~ Anita Swetman,UK

"Anyone who has left the security of their families and friends to live abroad will recognize themselves in Lisa's story."

~ Susan Hull, Sweden

"[*Dare to Dream* is] written in an entertaining way, exposing very well the challenges of expat life in France. Thank you for such a good read!"

~ Stéphanie Maurer, Ile de Re

"An easy to read account of perseverance and courage that inspires the reader."

~ Carolyn Parker, UK

"Every stage of her life was a learning experience captured by magical moments of love, laughter and dance. She inspires her readers to honour the feelings that migrate from the heart and to follow them, never settling for just living but to thrive with joy and love."

~ Rita Michel Greisse, UK

"*Dare to Dream* is a delightfully engaging, easy read. I have taken some of her motivational mantras to use within my own life. Whether you are interested in dancing or moving to France, or neither, it's a lovely memoir of a person's achievements, struggles and ultimate discoveries about themselves. Every reader will take away something from this book."

~ Holly Smith, UK

Never settle for second best
when you can follow your dreams
and create the life you choose...

Dare
to
Dream

Lisa Plutoni

First published by Fuzzy Flamingo 2022
Copyright © Lisa Plutoni 2022

Lisa Plutoni has asserted her right to be identified as the author of this
Work in accordance with the Copyright, Designs and Patents Act 1988.

ISBN: 978-1-7397850-3-1

Editing and design by Fuzzy Flamingo
www.fuzzyflamingo.co.uk

This book is dedicated to my Mum.
Thank you from the bottom of my heart for everything.
I know how much you love me and I always look up to your
shining example.
You will always be my greatest inspiration, Mum, and I love you.

Contents

"Between my first breath
and my last breath,
everything in between belongs to me,
it's my life"

~ Lisa Plutoni

Introduction

I was in intensive care. I had never felt more alone in my entire life. What was I doing here in a foreign country, far from my family and in a hospital completely alone... what was going on?

I wish I had listened to my body. I knew I had to ease up on something, but what? I was on my own bringing up my two boys in a foreign country and there were so many major decisions to make. What could I ease up on? I distinctly remember thinking this just a couple of days before I ended up in casualty with a blood clot in the centre of my brain!

I was stripped of every piece of clothing, jewellery and mobile phone. I was completely naked. I felt like a tiny being in a foreign environment with this dreadful feeling of being so totally alone. What happened next was a whirlwind, I don't remember much.

My best friend Sam, bless her, looked after my kids and I found out later that there was some sort of volcanic ash cloud, so all airports were closed. Mum and Dad finally arrived by train from England and I was so emotional I set off all the alarms and within seconds had a handful of nurses come running to my bedside! I remember saying, 'It's okay, *I'm alive!*'

It was 2010, a year I'll never forget, and it was a year that changed my life forever.

But first, let's go back to the beginning…

1. Back to My Roots
Birth to Age Seven

I was born in 1964 at St Mary's hospital in Coleraine, Northern Ireland. My dad was in the RAF, so we didn't stay there long; even all those years ago, we were already travellers. My first name is Lisa, which is what I have always used, but I was christened Elizabeth and my maiden name is Thomas. My parents were Welsh but apart from happy family holidays camping in Snowdonia, I grew up in England. I left the UK for France when I was just twenty years old. Today, I describe myself as having Irish origins, Welsh blood and a French heart.

★★★★

My first memory is having my tonsils taken out. I was only three years old. I wasn't eating properly and, in those days, it was thought that removing my tonsils would make things better. I was in a cot with my teddy bear and there were two other bears, one big one and a baby one. I played Goldilocks and the three bears. Years later, when I accidentally put my beloved bear in a bag and threw it out,

I was devastated. I still have three bears in my bedroom and now I guess they remind me of the comfort I found in the hospital when I was alone and only three years old. I also remember wanting a black walkie talkie doll. "Tessa" is 56cm, she walks and turns her head with each step and when you turn her over she cries "Mama". She has always been precious to me.

I started ballet classes when I was four years old in Stafford at the Wynne Porter Ballet School. My first dancing show was *The Wizard of Oz* in 1970. I took ballet and tap classes. I loved it right from the beginning. There is a very early photo of me wearing a yellow tutu and to my experienced eye today I can see that I showed talent. My parents didn't know then that I was to become a professional dancer.

As a child, I changed schools a lot. I was always the new girl and I remember always having to fit in. When I was five years old and the new girl at school, I painted a blue snowman because I had come to school and it was closed, so I was waiting for my mum to pick me up. I remember my first boyfriend Paul Quick and giving him a hundred kisses sitting on the steps at school.

My grandparents ran a pub and I used to eat crisps and pop – which is what we called fizzy drinks – behind the bar. I would go with my nan to play bingo and I loved the excitement of winning a game when I would nudge my nan who would shout out, 'Bingo!'

At this time, my dad was an aircraft engineer, so we moved from Stafford to Luton airport, which is where I remember spending most of my childhood. Nothing set me up to spend my adult life living in glamourous Monte Carlo!

When we moved to Luton, I was the new girl at dancing school, this time attending the Anne Gale School of Dance. This is where I would spend a good part of my childhood, in the basement studio of a large Victorian house, learning how to dance.

As a child I was obedient and one day at age seven, I found a sweet inside my school desk. Knowing that this was not allowed, I hid it in someone else's desk and then found out that it was for the tidiest desks, so I felt cheated!

Mum used to walk us halfway to school then we would continue on our own as there were no more roads to cross. At this time, Mum was taking in boarders, and she would cook a big English breakfast for everyone, so I always woke up to a delicious smell of eggs and sizzling bacon before school.

I have one sister. There are only fourteen months between us, so we grew up almost like twins, but we were like chalk and cheese. We both started dancing together but, as I continued, my sister went on to horseride and take swimming lessons.

Dad became a private pilot and he would do pleasure flights out of Luton Airport. He would waggle his aircraft wings as he flew over our house, so Mum knew to put the kettle on, because he would be home shortly. We had our own vegetable garden and Dad would take great pride in his green runner beans, and I loved digging up new potatoes.

I had a pet tortoise called Tobi and I would spend hours looking for him in the garden. We always had a dog too. Hobo was a stray dog who adopted us; we took him in and gave him a home. I remember my mum crying her eyes out on the first morning without him. No matter how heartbreaking it is to lose them, a dog would always be a vital part of my family. In my view, a house without a dog is not a home.

I had a happy childhood and I lacked nothing. My sister and I would often see my cousins Darren and Wayne and we would play for hours outside before the time came years later when mobile phones and computers would steal a child's youth and innocence.

I also remember going fishing with my grandpy, which I loved. They lived on a farm, and we would collect fresh eggs from the chickens and make dens in the haystacks. I am lucky to have such happy childhood memories.

2. Stage Struck
Eight to Fourteen

All my friends had solo dances but not me. I was eventually included in the group dances and my first experience on a big stage was as a little Korean angel in 1974. I was ten years old. We were invited to dance at the Royal Albert Hall in London in The All England Dance Festival Gala Performance. That was it, I was hooked. I loved the stage.

I finally got my first national solo and at age twelve I won the All England Dance competition. I was number twenty and I performed an Albanian dance. My skirt was made entirely of black braids stitched together, which took my mum hours and hours to make. It had to be heavy as I came on stage crouching like a bird. When they called my number, I didn't move and had to look down at my number card before realising that it was me who had won! It was such a happy and proud moment. It was the first time I had ever won anything.

The following year, I came second, then at age fourteen I won the prestigious Garrard Cup again and I was even in my local paper. I felt like I was getting somewhere.

Even in those days, dance classes weren't cheap. Mum and Dad invested in my classes, not to mention making all my costumes and travelling up and down the country with me to participate in dance festivals. I had no idea of the expense. In those days, as a child, it was just something that I did, carefree, with no regard of the cost.

When eventually I was given my first ballet solo (way later than everyone else), my mum admitted that she was losing hope in me ever getting the chance and if I didn't get a ballet solo soon maybe I should stop dancing. I came home that evening smiling and so proud to announce that I had my very own ballet solo. That day, I knew that Miss Gale, my ballet teacher, believed in me.

I remember performing my first ballet solo as a novice at Filey Dance Festival. As I stood centre stage, waiting for my music to begin, my legs were visibly shaking. I was so nervous. Once the music started, I was off, and all nerves were forgotten as I danced my heart out. I gained first place.

I continued to shine. I now had solos in every category. I won all of my novice sections and suddenly overnight everything clicked; I just got it! One day, I just knew how it felt to move my body and from that day on I never looked back. Each week, I got better and better and gained confidence. Even my teachers were surprised at my progress, and it felt like overnight everything they had been teaching me made sense and there was no stopping me now.

I was a Jenny Babe in a professional pantomime, which came to Luton Library over Christmas, and I remember having to come out of school to rehearse, which was so exciting. I had a child's contract, which made me feel very grown up and I loved it. The following year, I became a Jenny set dancer with the other girls my age. At last, I had proved myself and moved up with them; I was so grateful.

★★★★

At home, I always felt loved, although we weren't a family who kissed or hugged a lot. I have happy childhood memories. Christmas was always magic. My dad was the perfect Santa and we had traditional Christmas rules, which absolutely had to be abided by. We were spoiled rotten with way too many gifts, lacking nothing, but the highlight was our Christmas tree game, originally started by my grandfather. It was a numbers game. We would pick a number out of Santa's special box then search for the gift hidden somewhere on the Christmas tree. We always had a huge bushy Christmas tree, and it was a very special treat the day we would go out as a family to choose our tree. Dad would put the lights on first then my sister and I were allowed to add the decorations. We would go to church on Christmas morning then come home and open our presents one by one. Mum always made a fabulous traditional Christmas dinner and I remember it was always such an exciting day.

In France, Christmas Eve is the most important day, although I still keep up my British traditions of celebrating on Christmas Day. On Christmas Eve, we sit down for a lovely meal and open one present each before getting a good night's sleep waiting for Santa to come.

Occasionally I'd do it the French way and hated it. The kids would fall asleep in the middle of the party and on Christmas morning when all the magic is supposed to happen everyone would be sleeping off their indulgence of the night before. I vowed never to do it again.

Now my sons are adults, we do enjoy Christmas Eve, but the magic still happens the next day when we open our stockings, and we all turn into big kids again. This year, my eldest son has a flight on the 26th, so we'll FaceTime him and, of course, my mum and sister in England. When you live overseas, there are many events when you miss your family. It never gets any easier and often I feel like I am in the wrong place at the wrong time. It takes a conscious thought to remind myself that this was my choice and to stop punishing myself.

Family holidays were often camping, mostly in Snowdonia. Oh, how I loved getting up early in the morning to pick mushrooms in the fields for breakfast and then go for a swim in the river. We climbed Snowdonia and left our names on a little piece of slate at the top of the mountain.

During my childhood, I was kept busy dancing and my mum would spend hours waiting for me to finish class. I always danced, this is how I remember my childhood.

When I first went to France, I loved how everyone kissed each other. I vowed that I would do this with my own kids and tell them often how loved they were. Maybe this simple reason is why I wanted to have my kids in France.

Mum was always with me. She would spend hours sewing my dance costumes and she always encouraged me. I remember having a history project at school and Mum doing most of it for me as it involved following actual events in the news, cutting out newspaper articles and analysing the facts, but I was at dancing classes every evening and I wasn't interested at all in what was going on in the outside world.

My dad and I were often in conflict. I always felt that he treated me differently. Whatever I said was wrong, whatever my sister said was right. It hurt a lot. I know he loved me. He gave everything for me to get through dance college. I didn't get a county grant like most of the other students, and it was only because Dad had now qualified as a pilot and was working abroad earning good money that he was able to pay my fees. I loved him for supporting me and always showing me how to follow my passion.

Dad was destined for the Welsh mines, but he never gave up on his dream, he passed his private pilot's licence and then got his commercial pilot's licence. I didn't realise at the time what a huge achievement this was but what I do remember is his passion for everything he put his heart into.

We finally became much closer years later when I was a divorced single mum and needed help. When I broke my arm, he was the first one to jump on a plane and he drove me around for the two months it took to heal my arm. I felt really close to him then and we shared some happy weeks together.

With my kids I always tell them I love them and give them a kiss and a hug. It is the French way and part of their culture. Going to England with them as kids, they kissed everyone goodnight and Mum said how nice that was.

As there are only fourteen months between my sister and I, we grew up together, but we were very different. I was disciplined from an early age, I was always dancing and I knew exactly what I wanted to do. My sister was constantly changing her mind about what she wanted to do, one minute it was swimming and the next it was horses. She was into the music scene and would go to punk concerts, which I never really understood. She eventually decided to study art and became a very successful make-up artist, travelling and making much more money than me. She is a better businesswoman than me.

My kids are much older than hers, so we didn't share bringing up our children together, which I feel sad about. In fact, it probably created more distance between us as well as the fact that I was in another country. We often didn't understand each other and yet we seem to have grown closer as we age. I like to think that we can develop a closer relationship as we grow older, and I thank her for always being there when I needed her. When I split up from my first husband and I was trying to get my mortgage accepted by my bank, my sister paid off my car so that the bank would agree to give me the mortgage and I will always be grateful for that. My boys always loved their aunt, and she would spoil them rotten with the latest gadgets and toys when they were little. We've both been through ups and downs in our marriages, but blood is thick and there is no doubt that we will always be there for each other.

3. The Good Old Days
Fifteen to Twenty-One

At age fifteen, I went to Ilkley Ballet Seminar and was taught by the wonderful dancers Dame Alica Markova and Anton Dolin. I felt very honoured. I continued to perform in pantomimes and got my professional Equity card at age sixteen. I loved it all. By seventeen I was doing Hollywood Music Hall with Diana Dors and we had an exciting trip to London to dance at the Tower Bridge Hotel escorted by our two teachers.

I loved my dancing teacher Miss Gale. She gave me the chances I so desperately wanted and believed in me. In 1981, when she died of leukaemia aged forty-three, I was devastated. It was my first funeral and I fled from the church.

"May knowing that so many people share your grief help to comfort you in this time of sorrow" were the words on our sympathy card but as a child I just didn't understand it.

★★★★

Life went on and I continued to dance with Miss Anne, who was more technical and quite scary at times, but she was a good teacher. At seventeen, I was a finalist for the Cosmopolitan Young Dancers Award, and I won a year's scholarship for the prestigious Pineapple Dance Studios in London. I was so excited. This is where all budding dancers would go to class and I went there as often as I could, taking the train from Luton to London. I would watch the older girls auditioning knowing that one day it would be me.

I had a strawberry party for my eighteenth birthday. We had strawberry desserts everywhere. I remember having a lot of fun. I was so innocent, not like eighteen-year-olds today who seem to know it all and have so much confidence.

When I left school, I already had my professional performers Equity card, so I decided with my parents that the sensible thing to do was teacher training. I auditioned for London College of Dance and Drama, which was the ISTD teacher training college founded in 1944 by Grace Cone and Anita Heyworth. Madge Atkinson and then in my days Phrosso Pfister were principles and I had teachers such as Jacqueline Ferguson (RAD), Mirella Bartrip (Modern), Joan Darwall (Greek), Richard Glasstone (National), Anita Heyworth (Natural Movement) and last but not least Michelle Scott, who taught me Matt Mattox Jazz, which I enjoyed so much.

In 1983, I was one of four dancers selected to perform at the University of Surrey and we presented a revival of old Natural Movement dances. It was an honour and privilege. I excelled thanks to Miss Gale, I felt like I was doing her an honour as well as making history and being coached by Anita Heyworth. I must also mention my wonderful Greek dance teacher Joan Darwall who was over eighty years old but she taught me so much about movement and was such an inspiration to me.

My college life was wonderful. I have such happy memories. I loved London College, which was actually in Bedford, and I had my own flat, which I shared with two other girls. We had such a fabulous time. There wasn't anything else I wanted to do. I loved my classes; I loved performing on stage and learning teaching skills, anatomy and the history of dance. Every day was a gift, it was magic. The friendships I made at college have lasted a lifetime and every ten years we all meet up for a reunion, which is exciting, and everything feels like yesterday again.

★★★★

So, let's talk now about what attracted me to France.

I first came to France on a French exchange trip when I was thirteen and, from that day on, I was hooked. It felt exciting and special. I loved learning the language. I have always liked new things and being different; it is part of my family genes. We are leaders, we like discovering new places and adventures. My parents were often abroad in some exotic location and their travelling lifestyle has certainly rubbed off on me.

I was in Compiegne, Oise, in a beautiful villa with a pool and I loved it. I made countless mistakes in my

French, but I didn't care, I was learning and living a French lifestyle. We would go off on our bikes into the forest and I felt such a sense of freedom and happiness. I loved the French marketplaces, which would stay with me for many years. Even today there is nothing I enjoy better than wandering around a local market full of colourful fruits and vegetables, baskets, spices, utensils made from olive wood, floppy sun hats, olive oils, wine and vast selections of cheeses. All my senses come alive, and I feel vibrant and glowing.

The highlight of my trips to Compiegne was a day out to Tati, the historic shop, boulevard Rochechouart in Paris. Oh, the excitement. I loved Tati! Everything was affordable and we would come home with bags of new clothes, belts, bags and new shoes. It was always a perfect day out. I was so sad when Tati closed many years later and with it some of my fond childhood memories.

France was so much more exotic than the boring UK. At home it was grey and always raining and I dreamed of living in France. I was naturally attracted to anything French and, of course, my first love was a French man. We were just kids, I was young and carefree and I fell in love; it was the start of a long romance. Everyone was against it. He was three years older than me and not considered a serious guy with a proper job, but what did I care? He was gorgeous, handsome and sexy. We had our first intimate relationship when I was seventeen and it was oh so very sweet. I was head over heels in love with him.

I remember joining a class at the local dance school

and the first time he ever saw me dance was to the song "Can't Take My Eyes Off You" by Frankie Valli and the Four Seasons. I felt amazing, so special and so loved, everything was perfect. I knew this was it; I wanted to have my children in France and I wanted France to become my home. As I grew up from a child to a young woman, he was always there for me, and I felt loved and cherished.

My boy-friend was there when I graduated from London College of Dance and Drama in 1984 and my diploma day marked the fortieth anniversary of the college. My friends and family shared this wonderful day with me, and I felt on top of the world. I knew that my wildest dreams were about to begin.

When I left college, I was twenty and I was offered a teaching job in Amiens, France, at a local RAD ballet school. It was going to be perfect, and I wanted to be with my man. In reality, my contract was too restrictive, so I didn't sign it, but decided instead that I would give classes in the small surrounding villages. My boyfriend and I moved into a house together with our white cat Julie. We had nothing, just a mattress and a table with two chairs and a fireplace. With a banking ban, things were not looking good. We were not allowed to borrow any money and we were not getting anywhere. I realised that I wasn't prepared to give up my dreams for such a gloomy future. When he started asking me about what interior decoration, curtains and bedspreads I liked, I realised that I had so much more to do with my life. I wasn't ready to settle down.

I moved down to the South of France and auditioned

for a dance company. We rehearsed every day, but I found out that we only got paid if we did a gala. This wasn't going to work, so I auditioned as a teacher by teaching a jazz class and was offered work in a reputable dance centre, which today is a highly acclaimed dance centre in Montpellier. I started to teach jazz dance with real live djembe musicians. I loved it but I wasn't ready to teach, I wanted to dance, so I made the decision to return to Paris. I auditioned to join the prestigious Mermoz luxury cruise ship and the next thing I knew, I was back in the South of France boarding the ship.

My childhood romance lasted until my twenty-first birthday. He met me on the Mermoz cruise ship in Toulon and gave me twenty-one red roses as I told him that I was ending our relationship. I had dreams, I had much more exciting things to do than get married, I had the world to visit, and this is exactly what I did as I sailed away into the sunset.

★★★★

This was where my career as a professional dancer really began and I knew that I had done the right thing. I loved sailing, I loved living on board and visiting a different port every day. It was magical. I was earning good money and doing what I loved. I would dance three shows a week, rehearse and live like a tourist the rest of the time. It was an amazing contract. I was happy, I loved travelling and I was living my dream as a professional dancer. Our choreographer was Jean Guelis, our numbers were comic and the themes were often about life onboard.

I guess most little girls want to dance. Maybe I could have been a ballerina but it was jazz I really loved. I loved the rhythmical music, the flashing lights and the glittering costumes. I won a scholarship for White Lodge Ballet Summer School in 1984 and yes I enjoyed it but after a week I was outside waiting for my jazz teacher to pick me up ready to take me to my jazz summer school!

When I was jazz dancing, it felt so good, and that's how I went from ballet shoes to jazz shoes and heels to becoming a professional dancer. I always listened to my heart, I didn't think twice and I was spontaneous, always following my intuition. Even today, I have absolutely no regrets. I would do everything I did all over again. Before leaving on the cruise, I had auditioned for the prestigious contemporary school in Angers. I had a satellite message come through that I had been accepted but I decided that I had done enough training and I was now ready to dance and see the world!

As a kid, I always wanted to dance, and Mum says it's all I ever wanted to do, but I don't actually remember sitting down and contemplating my career. I just danced. It's what I did. I considered myself average at school, so maybe I thought I was never good enough to learn anything academic, but I have proved myself wrong by becoming a lifelong student. I am always learning something new, fascinated by new ideas and I've got some great qualifications, even with distinctions, which have proved to me that I am academically good enough.

4. Having the Time of My Life
Twenty-Two to Twenty-Eight

Dancing professionally was exciting. I loved it. I loved being on stage and performing. I loved rehearsals and behind the scenes even more than the show itself and my dancing years were the happiest of my life. I felt like I could do anything. I was confident and talented. I loved auditions, the thrill, the anticipation; I was in the right place at the right time doing what I was supposed to be doing. It just felt right.

I was twenty-one, cruising up North through the Norwegian Fjords. I visited Tromso, Norway, the Black Sea, Odessa, floated in the Red Sea, visited the blue mosque in Istanbul, the pyramids in Egypt and Mykonos in the Greek Islands. It was amazing. I was thrilled with every moment. The Spitzberg was stunning. I took snapshots with my little Kodak 126 camera but was so glad years later that I had bought some of the fabulous professional photos of the amazing icebergs and glaciers. I had no idea how lucky I was.

I loved visiting the local towns in Norway and even went to Iceland with the hot water geysers, which was exciting. After the visits I would return to the ship and feel truly at home. I had only myself to think about it's true, but even so, my life at such a young age was truly incredible. I had no idea how good it all was at the time, but I enjoyed every moment.

★★★★

In 1985 I was back in Paris and now I wanted to get into one of the huge Parisian revues. Not the Moulin Rouge (too many feathers) nor the Crazy Horse (too naked for me) nor the Lido (I was too small) but Paradis Latin, which had more dancing. Molly Molloy was a fabulous renowned choreographer. It was my second audition in Paris after the cruise ship and there was a lot of competition. I had strong classical ballet training, and this always helped me in auditions. If you want to dance, start with ballet, it gives you the basis to do everything else. I loved auditions, found them easy and I always got the job. I joined Paradis Latin and our revue "Champagne" was wonderful. I absolutely adored it all. I loved the choreography, the costumes, the lights, the music, my life as a dancer. I was in love with Paris.

I rented a tiny room on the top floor of a big house, and I had a huge terrace overlooking the rooftops of Paris from Le Sacré Coeur across to the Eiffel Tower in the distance. I was in heaven, carefree and loving everything I did.

I used to go to classes every day in Pigalle where all the dancers hung out and then I performed in the evenings. Paradis Latin was like a huge family and on 31st December

1985 there was nowhere else I wanted to be more than just where I was. It was magical.

★★★★

Little did I know, but my dad had a serious health condition. It wasn't like today when you could just send an email or chat over FaceTime. I don't even remember having a mobile phone or in fact any phone at all. Apparently, my mum had written a letter, but I never got it. That's another thing in France; your name has to be on the letterbox, as you won't get any letters with just the address. Anyway, I was not aware of what was going on back home and just how serious my dad's health was. I was up on stage performing every night and enjoying my career. When I eventually realised what was going on back in England, I asked to leave. I was under contract, but they let me go for medical reasons when I told them about my dad, and I returned hastily to the UK.

Dad had already had a major operation – a heart bypass – and now he was recovering. Where had I been all this time? I was furious, how come no one had told me? I hadn't known what was going on! I felt betrayed, alone, treated like a foreigner; all I wanted was to be at home now.

Dad recovered, and life continued. I don't remember much about this period. I felt like I didn't fit in again. I remember being drawn back to France. I arrived in Paris and gave myself three weeks to get a new job.

★★★★

Auditioning for Monte Carlo was like no other audition. It lasted a whole two days. Every dancer in Paris was there, everyone wanted the job. I did what I had to do, I was professional and I was good at it. After two solid days of auditioning with the best dancers all eager to get this prestigious contract, I was chosen! I couldn't believe it! ME! Wow! I was so thrilled and excited. OMG I was going to Monte Carlo!

This turned out to be my best contract ever and one of my happiest summers. The work was intensive and in such a beautiful location on the beach, it was perfect. The open-air Sporting d'été overlooked the sea and our shows were amazing. We danced all day rehearsing and getting tanned on the beach, totally relaxed, enjoying every day and, of course, falling in love with this way of life. I was in top shape and nothing was stopping me.

Here I was, a Monte Carlo dancer at the famous Salle d'Étoiles in Monaco, the gala performance of le Bal de la Rose in the presence of royalty in the summer season of 1986. What a year that was! It sounds exotic and believe me it was. Lydie Callier was our choreographer, and our costumes were made to measure on the very top floor of Monte Carlo's famous casino; I felt like a princess. It was all so magical, every single part of it. I remember my parents flying out to see the show and how proud they were. I shared a flat with my friend, which turned out to be one of the longest lasting friendships of my life. We may not see each other for years and then pick up from where we left off as if it were yesterday. These friendships are one of the greatest gifts of life. My dancing friends often became my best life friends.

★★★★

Not only did we perform a fabulous show but, during this long summer of 1986, I met my first husband and the father of my children. In those days, I could have had anyone I wanted, but I steered away from the rich millionaires with their fancy cars. I thought they would treat me like a princess, use me then reject me. I did have dinner one evening with HRH Prince Albert, Princess Stephanie and a couple of friends, but I wasn't attracted to money. I preferred the genuine locals who lived and worked there, the honest workers, and so I fell for my ex. He was a waiter in one of the late-night restaurants, the Bistroquet, which stayed open all night. We would go there to eat after the show. His charm worked on me, and I was hooked.

I remember Lydie saying, 'Ooh, be careful, lots of dancers fall in love and never leave!' and I thought no not me, but although I did leave, I did come back to the dazzling life in Monaco.

My career, however, was not finished yet. I auditioned for Japan and even though I was too small and almost left the audition feeling mad, I actually got the job. I remember flying to Tokyo on my own and being the only European on the flight. When I arrived, I was met by a young Japanese boy who was holding my name up and he whisked me away in a taxi. I mean, he could have been anyone, but I felt no fear at such a young age. He took me to a tiny little dressmaker's shop, and I was measured from head to toe for costumes all made brand new just for me.

I loved Tokyo. I loved the French tearooms and the Japanese baths. I'd go in and be given a small bucket to take a cold shower then I would step into a hot bath to soak before repeating the ritual. I would come out feeling revived and on top of the world.

After Japan, I toured Italian theatres with an operetta company and I only saw my boyfriend a couple of times. I remember meeting him on the border of France and mixing up English, French and now Italian. I couldn't get a sentence out in the right language and this was such a weird experience, I'd heard of but never experienced before.

I remember dancing at the National Theatre in Milan one day then travelling in our tour bus right down to Reggio Calabria in the South. I remember rehearsing then wanting to join my friends on the beach. I took a local bus but got totally lost and when I got off and asked about the return trip, I was told that the next bus back to town was the next day. I panicked. I had a show that night. Where on earth was I? An old Italian woman took me back to her house, but I remember thinking that she was more like a witch and I just had to get out. I eventually convinced her in my pigeon Italian that I needed to get back to town and she took me back to the station. There I met a kind old lady who looked after me, paid my ticket and said she lived next to the theatre. I was so relieved. We got back safely and I invited her to come and see the show that evening. Never have I been so grateful.

After this contract, I decided to go home and I got a job in the West End, London. My boyfriend followed me to London, and he did well for himself getting a job as manager of the Hilton restaurant. We had a lovely apartment in West Hampstead and one day he proposed. I was twenty-six and I said yes. After all, surely it was time to get married now and settle down? I was excited, I chose a beautiful dress with a veil, and we planned to marry in England then move to France to settle down.

★★★★

So, at twenty-six years old, here I was, getting married, not to my first love (who was much too sexy), but to my charming waiter who was French with Italian origins. Someone who I had decided would be the perfect husband, loyal and stable. Besides, it was time I got married, right? This is what girls my age did. I was ready to give up my career as a professional dancer, move to France and settle down, just as I had planned I would, and now that time had come.

I returned to France married and we made our home in Menton between Monaco and the Italian border. I was happy. I had followed my dreams, danced my way around the world and now I was ready to settle down and unpack my suitcases.

★★★★

Living in France always felt exciting, thrilling and special. I learnt real French in France, not the French vocabulary we learn at school and then never use. I even failed my French exam at school because I guess I was using slang words, so I got disqualified. I was horrified, it was my favourite subject! I pleaded with my French teacher to allow me to resit my exam and I applied myself with correct grammar and vocabulary and I got my grades. I was so relieved to pass!

★★★★

I always feel like an alien, even today when I speak fluent French; I just never quite seem to fit in. I know how it feels to meet a complete stranger, someone who is British, and I'll have a flowing conversation with them where everything familiar comes back in seconds. It's like being on the same wavelength, even if I don't know them, I feel at ease and comfortable. In France, I speak French, yes, but with errors like the feminine and masculine pronouns, which I don't think I'll ever get right. But it's okay. I think in French and communicate well. It's fine, it's just not my mother tongue and I never quite fit in with a crowd of people.

I don't know what I was trying to prove, moving to France, why did I do this? Why was I always attracted to France? I didn't think of the consequences, I just did it. I have always been spontaneous, letting my heart rule, leaping into the unknown, confident that I could handle whatever I was confronted with. I guess I could have chosen an easier way. But staying in England was never really an option for me, my mind was made up from a very early age. As I look back, I can't say I regret my decision, but I have no idea why I did it. I felt attracted to the lifestyle, I wanted to be like the French, I remember that. Maybe I thought they were chic and elegant, I don't know what it was, but I identified with them. Life in France has its ups and downs, nothing is easy and everything is different to England. Be warned, it takes a long time to settle in. One of the reasons for writing this book was for anyone thinking of moving here.

5. The Joy of Being a Mum
Twenty-Nine to Thirty-Five

I loved being pregnant. I was a glowing mum-to-be. Everything was perfect. I researched everything and knew exactly what to expect. I was going to be the perfect mum. From day one to giving birth it was magic. I was so happy, so fulfilled with love and joy. And Julien was the perfect baby; oh God he was beautiful. I was in awe of him. Was someone going to come and take him away? I couldn't quite believe how this perfect little boy was mine to keep. I came out of the maternity ward and went straight to the airport to pick up Mum and Dad who had come over to see their first grandson. I remember saying, 'Oh, close the car door quickly so that the air doesn't get on him!' What a funny thing to say. This always makes us laugh, even today.

I loved looking after my baby. It was a natural instinct, I would do anything for him, getting up several times in the night, nursing him to sleep and cradling him in my arms. I breastfed for ten whole months, I wanted to give my baby the very best start in life. I was ridiculously happy.

I had my second gorgeous son David three years

later. Where Julien was dark-haired with dark eyes and Mediterranean skin, David was blond with blue eyes and fair skin. They couldn't have been more different, and I was over the moon. The second time I gave birth, I felt it because the first time Julien had just slipped out effortlessly. I didn't have gas and air for either birth, I wanted to feel the experience and honestly both were fabulous. May 1995, I had two babies and I was the happiest woman in the world.

I was privileged to be able to stay at home and watch my babies grow. I loved being a full-time mum. My boys are the best accomplishments of my life. I was wonderfully happy.

★★★★

I eventually went back to part-time work, teaching tap dance at another prestigious dance school, this time in Nice chez Serge Alzetta, Centre Artistic Professional. I taught ballet in Menton chez Marie France Ceschel and tap chez Danielle Rovere. I even opened my own school "Dance Explosion" in Vintimiglia, Italy.

My kids were still toddlers and I hated leaving them. I did it for a year then I decided that it just wasn't worth it, I wanted to put my family first, so I came out of a declining partnership. I didn't speak fluent Italian and I didn't want to rent premises in Italy. I chose to put my family first.

We lived on the border. My ex-in laws were Italians. I loved the big family reunions and, of course, food was at the centre of everything. I started to learn Italian and got by as best I could. When all the family got together with everyone talking, I lost the conversation, but I didn't mind. I was happy being different. Besides, my kids were little, and they were my focus of attention. I always liked the idea of big families and everyone getting on together. This was my ideal vision but, in reality, it was a different picture, which I was to discover later on.

I insisted on getting both my boys baptised in Church of England churches. These were happy occasions and big family events, which I loved. We would go to a family restaurant and have countless courses of food from midday right into the early evening. There would be the apéritif, then antipasti, pasta, fish, meat, vegetables, dessert and coffee. It was never-ending and all delicious. These were such happy events.

I rarely went to church in France and certainly my husband wanted nothing to do with it, so my boys grew up without any formal biblical training. In school, they were the only ones not to do their confirmation at age eight because I believed it should be their choice. Since I had British nationality and I was a protestant rather than Catholic I chose for them not to do it at school. I still feel that it's really hypocritical to dress kids up as little white angels. In my church, when we are old enough, we may or may not choose to get confirmed. I did and my mum did, but my sister didn't and it was a personal choice. I was so proud when my dad got confirmed as an adult.

I have to say that I have drifted away from the church nowadays. The services I found in France were always so stuffy and I never knew the songs. My childhood church was lively; we had gospel singing, music and dancing, bonfire nights and church fairs, nothing like what I experienced in France. One day I volunteered to help at the church jumble sale in Menton and when the doors opened it was hell let loose. People just pushed, shoved and grabbed at everything, I hated it. I vowed never to do that again and I left the church. I didn't, however, leave my spirituality and today this means more to me than actually attending a church service.

Times change and so do we. Now when I go to church it is in the UK in the village where my dad is buried. It still feels old and stuffy, and I miss my old St. Francis church, which was so much more fun.

★★★★★

My sons both played football. From age four, I remember trekking around the football stadiums every weekend to watch them play. I enjoyed it but sometimes it would be bitterly cold. They played in all weather, even in the pouring rain, and after a good ten years, I finally got tired of hanging around football stadiums in what was, after all, a rather masculine atmosphere. I did it for my boys and often I would take other children with me too. When they were teenagers, my boys did cycling and then running and I loved that they were sporty. Much later, when David was twenty-one, he finished the ultra-trail of Mont Blanc, which was 170km. This was such a wonderful experience for all of us, so full of raw emotions, pride and joy. Oh God, I thought my heart would break at times, I was so proud of him. I treasure these memories.

6. Losing Myself
Thirty-Six to Forty-Two

By thirty-six, I had two fabulous sons, a beautiful house and a dog. I was a stay-at-home mum and loved it, but my marriage had gone stale. It wasn't that anything was really bad – from the outside it certainly looked perfect – but I was unsatisfied and unhappy. It wasn't what I wanted.

How do you keep a relationship from becoming stale? Well, I believe that there has to be love, admiration and excitement. I liked the idea of being in love and maybe I was in the beginning, but it wore off and I became bored. Our relationship was too stable, too predictable and I wasn't "in love" any more. I began to hate the feeling of never feeling satisfied. I wanted so much more.

I hadn't really given any thought about my perfect partner, just like I didn't think of becoming a dancer, I just followed my heart. Getting married was the same; I didn't think about it or plan it as some girls do. I just followed my heart and instincts, only now they were telling me that I needed something different. I felt that I was cheating on myself by settling for second best, which I definitely wasn't going to let happen.

I needed to vibrate; I needed to feel loved and understood. I have a passionate nature, it had to feel right, I wanted to be head over heels in love and I realised that I wasn't. I wanted so much to fit in, but I realised that I was, in fact, losing my identity.

My sons, of course, were the best thing that had ever happened to me, yet I felt more and more uncomfortable. I was losing myself and losing my self-confidence. I was always considered a foreigner, I used to do what I thought I was supposed to do, but no matter how hard I tried, I never quite fit in. I was always an alien.

It isn't always easy to live in a foreign country. First of all, you are far from family, your roots and everything that feels familiar. The strange thing is that, after making my life in France, when I went back to England so much had changed from my childhood, I felt like a stranger there too. I felt like I didn't belong in either country. Even my family called me the Frenchie, which really hurt me as I was struggling to grasp my roots and I felt lost between both countries, not belonging to either.

I wanted a daytime job, close to home, which fitted in with my kids, so I began teaching dance and English at a private school La Villa Blanche in Menton. When I was at school, my mum used to be our school secretary and I loved having her close by. I too loved having my kids in my classes, the English work was fun, I enjoyed it and I even got Royal Academy of Dance ballet examinations going, which was a miracle as, not only did I have to teach the children, but educate the parents too. During this time my youngest son passed his primary exam and I also passed my Associate teaching exam with Distinction which made me so proud.

Meanwhile, my marriage was going from bad to worse. I was so tired of feeling tired. I wanted to feel in love. I wanted to feel special. I needed so much more than my ex was able to give me. It just wasn't enough for me. I refused to settle for less and the worst thing was he wouldn't communicate with me. In a desperate plea, I went to see a lawyer. I just needed a reaction from him. He wasn't ready to accept that our marriage was over, but he didn't do anything to make it better.

I told him outright that I wanted a divorce. I wanted to live, 100%, I wanted to vibrate like the true free spirit I was. I wanted so much more than he could give me. I tried but I just couldn't fake it. We'd probably both made mistakes, nobody is perfect, but it was over. I didn't love him anymore. I had to get out of this relationship.

As my boys grew into their teens, it wasn't always easy. They fought as most kids do. One was always competitive, and the other was never good enough for him. I was exhausted and often alone. My ex worked shifts. At mealtimes I was alone and at bedtimes too. It was okay, I didn't mind. My kids are everything to me. I no longer felt safe. I was scared, he just wasn't trying to make anything better. He just didn't seem to care enough. It was my lawyer who eventually told me to cut off the bad branches to allow myself to grow fully and this is the advice that I finally took.

★★★★

I had given up my job to become a full-time mum and, at the age of forty, I found myself out on a limb, a single mum in a foreign country with no family around to offer me any support. What was I going to do?

Being a fighter, I realised that the cliché "when the going gets tough, the tough get going" was true and I had to sort myself out. I didn't want to leave France, my boys were French, their father was French, I had decided to live in France, and I had wanted the divorce. I was drowning but now I had to take responsibility for my actions, get my act together. Besides, England felt distant and I felt strangely like an alien there too!

As a mum, you can't give up, you have to keep going. My school job had ended when the principle retired and the new one wanted to cut my wages in half, I had to find another solution to make ends meet. I had bills to pay, food to buy. I had no formal qualifications – I was a professional dancer, and no one was interested that I could do the splits or a double pirouette. It was a joke. At my age, women were now in corporate jobs, they were the leaders and here I was facing the dilemma of starting from scratch. To be honest, I felt way out of my comfort zone. I just didn't know how I was going to do it.

I had trained for years as a dancer. I had learnt discipline, and this turned out to be my saving grace. I wasn't giving up, I deserved better, and it was my strength of character that pulled me through the rough times. I was determined to make things work out. I convinced myself that I had what it took, I was strong and I had to pull my life together. I had to stay in France. There was no question of that. And I had to make things work out for my boys.

It wasn't easy, I almost lost the plot! I went from being a confident young girl who could do anything to a woman who didn't know which way to turn. I was almost at breaking point. If I didn't get a job, any job, that was it, I would have to leave France and go home to my parents. But that would be unfair on my boys. No, it was out of the question! I had to pull myself together and find a solution!

I was desperate, I would have done anything. I started working in a local supermarket but, on my first day, I got the job I really wanted in an international school. I had talked my way into it, I had made myself believe that I could do it, then I convinced others that I could do it too. I became a school secretary, just like my mum had done; the difference was that my mum was an expert. I didn't have a clue, I had never worked on a computer, I didn't know Word or Excel, but I told myself that I would learn, and I did. It turned out to be a stepping stone which saved me.

After a couple of years at the international school, I wanted to earn more money, so I applied for a secretarial position at one of the biggest companies in Monaco. Colin gave me the break I needed. He liked me, he told me "we both know that you are not a secretary" but he believed in me. He took a chance on me and offered me the job. I was so grateful.

I was out of my comfort zone again. I had never been a personal assistant but, realising the opportunity which had been given to me, I was going to make this work and so I did. I learnt on the job, I became good. I made the deadlines, and I had a good eye for detail and presentation. I was discreet and professional. Finally, I was earning a decent salary. I had my head above water. I never had a lot of money but now I had enough to make ends meet.

I learnt to take control of my own destiny. I knew that if I worked hard, I could learn anything and I started to get my confidence back. I was now working in English in an international company and at last I felt like I had found my place in Monaco. I had been living for years so close by in Menton; I should have come here years ago. In Monaco it was multilingual, I belonged here.

Don't let anyone ever tell you that you are not good enough. Life is about taking chances, seizing opportunities and believing in yourself. I had found myself again and life was getting better. I enjoyed my work, I enjoyed being part of a team, having lunch with the girls and organising international seminars. I felt like I belonged, that I was giving value and I started to shine.

My boys were growing up. I was finally making a decent salary and could support my family. It was really hard at times. I didn't feel guilty for leaving my husband because I don't believe parents should stay together for the sake of the children, but I didn't ever feel good enough. I wanted to give them so much more. I tried my best to be the best mum ever. I remember feeling desperate when Julien was fourteen, but by sixteen he had settled down again. We had so much fun on his sixteenth birthday! They were good kids, I never had to worry about alcohol or drugs, they were into sports, and I loved that. I had a reasonable relationship with my ex and the boys would come and go between us as they wanted. I was always there for them.

7. Nothing Could Have Prepared Me for What Happened Next
Forty-Three to Forty-Nine

Moving to France. If I could press rewind, would I do it all over again? What is it that I really love about France anyway?

Well, market day is a truly wonderful experience. I love it. I love the colours, the bustle, the smells, the noises, the wonderful array of fresh fruits and vegetables, the colourful baskets, spices, cheeses and wines. I love tasting foods and mixing with the locals. I feel in my element joyfully filling up my basket and buying fresh bread and caramelised onion slices. If I am lucky, I will sit at a terrace and have a cup of coffee, doing what the French do best, watching the world go by. Nowadays, as a couple, I just seem to get things done as quickly as possible and there is no coffee break as we head off home. But, if I'm on my own, I take my time, look at everything, take time to chat with the stallholders and sample their produce and I thoroughly enjoy myself.

Trying to do things in France as you would do in England is just a waste of time. You might just as well adapt from day one, which is what I did. I never mixed with expat groups until I was well into my fifties and, even then, I was disappointed. I much prefer to jump in the deep end with the locals. However, be warned: everything is different!

It took me ages to get around to the fact that the French considered potatoes a vegetable. Where I grew up it was meat, potatoes and two veg, so I would ask, 'Where are the vegetables?' and be told, 'We have potatoes.' No, I don't think so!

I picked up driving on the wrong side of the road easily enough, no problem. As Mum says, 'Just make sure the steering wheel is in the centre of the road.' Brilliant, sorted.

Plug sockets are all different, so don't bring any electrical appliances with you, it's just not worth it. You'd have to change all the plugs or use adaptors, so it's just easier to buy here.

Now I know some people love their cars and want to bring them over, but in a word: don't. The steering is all on the wrong side, the motorway tolls are all on the wrong side, and you'll have no privacy. I came over in a Renault 4 with British number plates and wherever I went people would know where I was and where I lived. I felt as if my every movement was tracked. People I didn't even know knew everything about me. I got rid of it as quickly as possible. If you're coming to live, buy a car here!

★★★★

So that was my life. I was in a nine-to-five office job. Ten years later, sitting behind a desk all day was taking its toll.

Looking back, I guess I was also eating for comfort, trying to deal with my divorce and trying to do everything on my own. I was no longer exercising, I had put on weight, I was tired of feeling tired and making all the decisions. I knew I had to give myself a break, but I didn't know what I could do, everything seemed to be so important.

★★★★

It was 2010…

I had such a throbbing headache, I felt like my head was going to explode. I was having such a good time too. Mum was visiting me and my boys, and she had just made one of her delicious chicken casseroles. As I was serving it up, I had to run to the bathroom and I was violently sick. I pulled myself together and immediately felt much better and we had a lovely evening. Mum was leaving the next day. I went to the doctor and he gave me a prescription for migraine tablets. I had never had a migraine. That afternoon, I took Mum to the airport for another one of our goodbyes as she left for England and, as usual, I ended up in tears. It felt like my life was so full of goodbyes. Why was I living in a foreign country on my own with two boys when everyone I loved was in another damn country?!

The next day I went back to work. I had been off for six weeks already with a broken arm after a fall, a couple of steps off a ladder whilst painting my bedroom. I'd had to get on the back of a moped as my son drove me to the hospital cradling my aching arm. I never got on mopeds, but I had no choice.

My dad had been the first one to jump on a plane and rescue me. The house was a wreck. I was in the middle of painting my bedroom, my bed was in the middle of the hall and all my belongings were everywhere. When dad arrived, he fixed it all. I couldn't do anything. He helped me cook, looked after my two boys, finished my painting and put everything back into place. He was my hero, and I was forever grateful. He stayed with me for a good few weeks, driving me everywhere, and just being there for me. I had never felt so close to my dad. He was there when I needed him. That's what my dad did. He was a carer.

After that, I was happy to go back to my job. My comfort zone, as I now call it. My work colleagues were pleased to see me and my boss too. He asked how my arm was and I said that my arm was fine but that I had a throbbing headache.

My best friend called my office number to ask how I was. I sobbed on the phone and told her my head was killing me. She immediately said, 'I'm coming to get you.' I was incapable of making a decision; apparently my text message had been all muddled up, and when Sam came to get me, I was waiting downstairs. She took me straight to A & E and stayed with me, holding my hand and stroking my head. I had a head scan and they gave me immediate relief but the waiting for results seemed to take forever. I was keen to go home but I was stuck there, and Sam was still there with me. When the doctor finally said that they were transferring me to the neurology unit in Nice Hospital I couldn't understand it. Why? What was wrong with me? I felt fine. What about my boys? Sam reassured me that she would take care of them, and I was transported by ambulance to Nice.

I was stripped naked, my phone, my earrings, and all my clothing taken off. I was freezing. I was naked on a cold iron platform, shaking uncontrollably as they did an angiogram on me. I couldn't stop shaking; I must have been in shock.

After what seemed like endless tests, I was strapped up to a monitoring machine with wires all over me monitoring my heart, my head and basically keeping me alive. When I came to my senses, I was in intensive care. I had a blood clot in the centre of my brain. WTF! How did that happen? The doctors were afraid of bleeding and the care and attention I got was amazing. Of course, I was in France and our medical system is one of the best in the world. I was in good hands.

Suddenly, Sam was there again, bless her. She had followed the ambulance and she was with me the whole time. I am forever grateful to her for being there. She had taken care of my boys and phoned my boss to say that I wasn't coming back to work. She called my parents and told them that I was in intensive care. I can only imagine the panic they must have felt as they had only just arrived back home after visiting me.

I must have slept a lot but, when I was awake, I felt fine. I didn't know what all the fuss was about. The doctors took every precaution possible. I felt very alone. I had never felt so alone in my whole life! There was no one I could call, no one to come and visit me. Yes, Sam came with Julien who was going off on a school trip. 'Yes, go!' I reassured him; I would be fine.

I didn't realise then just how much danger I was actually in. David visited but he was younger and thankfully didn't know what was going on with his mum. I was grateful for that as I looked into his big blue eyes and reassured him that I was fine and would be coming home soon.

I was divorced, I was totally alone, I was in France. I had been dating and one of my ex-boyfriends came to visit me as he had already lost his wife to a cerebral accident and here he was, reliving the same event all over again. He vowed to look after me no matter what happened, but we were no longer dating and I didn't love him. All I wanted was my mum and dad.

I felt totally alone, isolated and yet I knew I was getting the best care ever. Once I knew that my boys were being looked after, I began to relax and let the doctors and nurses get on with it all. I had to pee several times a day in a bed pan but when I needed a number two it traumatised me. I was expected to sit in a chair with a plastic bag in it next to my neighbour. I couldn't do it. I was too young. I was embarrassed. Surely I could just go to the loo. I remember having a panic attack and my heartbeat was racing as I pleaded to use the bathroom, but they wouldn't even let me stand up, let alone walk. I cried myself to sleep.

Do you remember the volcanic dust cloud of 2010? All airports were closed. My parents couldn't get on a plane. My sister organised first-class travel for them by train, which took about two days. When they finally arrived at the hospital, the nurse said that they were out of visiting hours and my dad was left prowling like a lion as he waited to get in. They explained that they had just arrived as fast as they could from England and the nurses finally agreed that they could come in one by one to see me.

When I saw my mum walk in, I set off all the alarms. I don't know how many doctors, nurses and students ran into my room, ripped the bedsheets off my chest and started examining me. 'It's okay, I'm alive!' I kept saying. It was only my emotions that had set off all the alarms. I had never been so grateful to see my mum and feel safe again. When it was Dad's turn, the alarms all went off again but this time the staff knew what to expect and I cried and laughed.

I stayed in intensive care for ten days. I was eventually allowed to stand up and take a few steps but, honestly, I felt fine, and it was such a relief to sit on a proper loo again.

I was moved into a room with an elderly lady. She was paralysed from the neck down. I could see the fear in her little bright eyes. I used to sit by her bed and hold her hand until her visitors came. I had a lot of time to reflect. The feeling of being all alone haunted me. I would never again put myself in this situation. I decided that my life had to change.

I had no aftereffects, nothing. I was extremely lucky. The doctor showed me the X-ray of the blood clot in the centre of my brain and said it was a miracle that I had come out with no consequences.

I slept a lot, so I guess I needed to rest. I remember a friend phoning me and saying I heard that you had a stroke and I laughed and said, 'No, of course not!' I hadn't even realised myself what had happened. I certainly hadn't put a name to it. When I finally realised I'd had a stroke, I was even more scared. How could that have happened to me? I was young, in good health, why had this happened?

I was off work for a good six months; fortunately, I was financially stable by this time. Everything was covered by my insurance and all I had to do was rest and get better.

★★★★

I vowed in the hospital that I would never be alone again, and this was a promise I made to myself… so I started dating again. Just an occasional drink, a dinner here and there, then on 1st November 2010 I met Eric and the magic happened. It wasn't love at first sight, he was smoking, which wasn't on my list but we did laugh a lot and he turned out to be everything I needed. We were on the same wavelengths, had both been through a divorce and both had kids of similar ages. We both knew what we wanted and, more importantly, what we didn't want. I felt loved and cherished again. As we celebrated the 31st of December together with friends, I cried my eyes out. At last, I had put an end to what had been a traumatic year for me. Eric seemed to understand and just hugged me. It was what I needed. It wasn't long before he asked me to move in with him in Monaco. Now it was getting serious…

In 2012, Eric and I got married and it was one of the happiest days of my life. Everything was perfect. I was relaxed, even when my wedding ring hadn't arrived and, as we opened the front door to leave, there it was sitting on my doorstep. I was so excited. I had chosen a gorgeous wedding dress with Sam and my special family and friends were all going to be there. We got married in the town hall of Monaco up on the rock. We were relaxed and happy.

Our photos were taken in the beautiful St. Martin gardens of Monaco overlooking the Mediterranean Sea then we all set off into the Haut-Var where we had our holiday home. Our wedding night was in a hotel overlooking beautiful Lac St. Croix and it was perfect. When we arrived at midnight the sky was lit with stars, billions of stars, and the birds were singing. I was in heaven. We had champagne and strawberries for breakfast.

Our reception party was in our garden. It was such a wonderful day. A perfect summer's day and yet it was still only spring. I have so many happy memories of love and joy. Everyone who meant something to me was there. It was a perfect day for us.

★★★★★

The following year in 2013, nothing could have prepared me for what was to happen so suddenly. We'd just received a phone call, Eric told me to sit down and took my hand. 'Your dad has died.' These words will always haunt me, and I can still feel the stab of pain.

'No,' I said shaking my head, 'you've got it wrong, it was my grandmother, not my dad.'

'No,' he said, 'it's your dad.' I crumbled and howled, shaking. How was it possible? I was stunned.

Life would never be the same again. I would never smile or laugh again. How did this happen? When I think of Dad today, the tears flow instantly. I have so much to thank him for. I miss him more than anyone will ever realise. I felt such acute pain and thank God I had Eric to hold me.

It's funny but the last phone call I had with Dad it was as if he knew. He asked about everyone and made sure that everyone was okay. He said he was beginning to feel old, and we arranged a visit together to see his mum in Wales. It was the last time I spoke to him. I didn't even get a chance to say goodbye. It still hurts, even today.

Dad's funeral was hard; the music kills me every time. Mum was amazing, so strong for all of us. Our whole family was reunited in spite of our loss. Dad wouldn't have wanted it any other way. We made him proud.

It took me a good four months before I began to feel normal again. Life has this horrible way of just continuing as if nothing has happened, but light always prevails over darkness.

Eric and I kept our promise and went to visit my Ruby Nana in Wales. She is still alive as I write and is now 103 years old. She is a wonderful woman with twinkly eyes and a great sense of humour.

8. Just When My Life Was Back on Track
Fifty to Fifty-Six

Let's fast forward to 2015. Believe it or not, I am leaving my "superwoman" job. It's not for me, after all; I am not a secretary, I am just pretending to be an efficient businesswoman. What I really want to do is dance again. Well okay, maybe I am too old now to dance, but I can teach Pilates, so when the opportunity came I gave up everything and chose to put my health first.

I had money, I had taken a voluntary redundancy package from work, and I had security. I was remarried, in a happy, loving and supportive relationship and I had the most precious gift of all, which was TIME. My boys were growing up fast and it was time to start thinking of myself and prioritising my health.

I left my job, stepped out of my comfort zone and consciously chose to put my health first. You see, we always have a choice, my friends. Sitting at a desk for eight hours a day wasn't for me; I wasn't a secretary, I was just pretending, but it wasn't me. I had moved up from being a secretary to a personal PA for one of our managers. I was part of our emergency team and I studied for my NEBOSH qualification and even got distinction. I would show them that I was worthy. I became part of emergency training and then moved over to HR and, with my new boss, we created a talent development scheme within the company. I was happy, loved my job and had no intention to leave. But, when they brought out their first voluntary plan, it was too good to be true. I decided to leave, step out of my comfort zone again and focus on getting my health back.

★★★★

I went to train as a Pilates teacher in London. It felt like an essential part of who I am. Being in a dance studio makes me feel alive and well again. I worked hard, I loved going back to study and I travelled back and forth from Monaco to London to complete my training. I fell in love with the Garuda method. I discovered it at a weekend celebration of dance in London with James D'Silva and Alan Herdman. It was amazing, flowing and organic. I loved it and knew that I had found my new venture.

I qualified and became a Garuda coach, which I loved because it was Pilates, yoga and dance combined. It felt amazing. When I left my corporate job, I had three years of financial freedom and time to give myself and I didn't waste a day of these precious gifted years. It was like getting a second chance. I also worked a lot on self-development. I trained as a nutrition and lifestyle coach and the more I learnt the more I loved.

My wellness journey really started in 2015. I was desperate. I had put on weight and had to somehow lose it. I know today that smoothies are better than juices – we need all the fibre we can get to help digestion and the elimination of toxins – but, back then, I juiced for thirty days. Not only did I lose ten kilos, but I gained so much energy. The best thing about this period was the insight it gave me concerning my health. I was clean, I felt alive, I no longer wanted to put any junk into my body. For a while, I experimented with vegan foods. I joined a local vegan group and took a three-month vegan cookery course. I loved it and discovered a passion for creating wonderful colourful foods, which were healthy and nourishing me. I wanted to learn more, really understand what I was putting into my body. I enrolled to study for twelve months with the Institute of Health Sciences in Dublin. Every module taught me so much; I learnt the science behind food, new coaching skills and I knew now that I wanted to help others too. I had never been an expert in the kitchen but now I could cook healthy meals for my family, and I felt so much healthier. I had discovered a real passion. Once qualified as a nutrition and lifestyle coach, I discovered WILDFIT® and enrolled on their ninety-day program to change my relationship with food. Oh wow, it was incredible. I was discovering food psychology and how much our emotions are connected to what we eat. Creating this awareness was a huge insight and I decided to train as a WILDFIT® coach. Investing money and time into myself was my way of getting my health back and it was a natural decision to want to empower others to do the same. I wanted everyone to experience the benefits I had found.

I still doubted myself, at times I told myself that I was too old to train and start all over, but I did it anyway and, as usual, I was good at what I did. I committed 100% and I believed that I could do anything again. I was disciplined and did what I had to do to make a new life for me and my kids. This time it was different. I had the support of my husband; I was no longer alone.

★★★★

I set up my own wellness company in Monaco in November 2018. Finding studio space for my Garuda classes was a challenge, everything in Monaco was so expensive. I started classes in Menton just twenty minutes from Monaco in a wellness centre. The space was beautiful, and I felt hopeful. Everything was perfect.

Meanwhile, I was still qualifying to become a WILDFIT® coach. I loved it. I loved food psychology and the programme I would offer to my future clients.

In January I had started my first online trial class, but I had a terrible cough. On one Zoom call I coughed so much I lost my breath and had to gasp to breathe. I assumed that I had caught the flu like so many other people. Maybe I had fractured a rib from coughing so much. I saw my doctor, but blood tests were all negative. I planned to have an X-ray on my ribs.

Nothing could have prepared me for what happened next…

I couldn't breathe. I had what can only be described as contractions in my thoracic rib cage. Before I knew it, I was in A & E again. This time I had blood clots in both lungs and a 200% chest infection. I broke down and cried… why was this happening to me? What was wrong with me? OMG not again, was I going to die this time?

I was taken to a temporary hospital bed where the nurse put contention stockings on me. I didn't really know why. It was only later that I realised it all originated from a leg cramp in my calf and yes I had experienced a bad one a few days ago.

I was on oxygen for two weeks! My lungs were blocked, and my respiratory system needed assistance. I was put on antibiotics for the infection. My mouth dried up with the oxygen and my lips chapped. By the end of two weeks, I was pleading for them to reduce the oxygen. I had a sore throat. Because of my previous medical scare, they wanted to keep me in for more tests and it went on and on. I felt like a test specimen. I hated hospital food; it was all sugar, so how did they expect me to get better?! All I wanted to do was to go home and eat myself healthy again.

Eric, Julien and David came to see me and brought me healthy treats. My two best friends, Sam and Fabienne, came to visit too. I had access to my iPad and could speak to my mum by FaceTime and it was much better than the last time. I didn't feel isolated.

★★★★

Covid didn't exist then but today anyone who's had it knows what it is like not being able to breathe and I was scared. However, in true fighting "Thomas" spirit I convinced myself that I was invincible.

I coached my first nutrition students from my hospital bed; it was my trial class and part of my qualification, and I wasn't going to jeopardise my chances of qualifying. And besides, it kept me going. I loved what I was doing; even on oxygen I was helping people to change their lives for the better.

I couldn't understand why someone like me who was essentially healthy, working out, doing mindful movement and eating well could be in hospital. What was wrong with me? Nobody knew! All my tests were negative!

★★★★

In the hospital, I was next to the window. It was bitterly cold outside. I felt a chill coming through the window.

They had to move me, I had a lung infection, I couldn't risk catching a cold now. I felt a distinct coldness over my shoulder and neck. Even the doctor felt it and my neighbour in the next bed. I huddled up for the night, covering my neck with blankets. The next morning, my neighbour moved out and I asked to move away from the window. The following day, an elderly lady was brought in to share my room and she was placed next to the window. I felt guilty and I kept asking her if she felt a cold draft from the window, but she felt nothing.

Then I knew, in a flash and with certainty, that it was my dad. He was there with me that night. I had not slept well. I had felt the cold. But, in the morning, I had felt so much better, I was breathing better. The sudden realisation that it was my dad was like a bright light coming on. Even today, while writing this, tears are flooding down my face. I truly believe that my dad saved me that night. He was there for me, protecting me and making me get better. Why hadn't I realised it? I could have spoken to him instead of complaining about the chilliness but that morning I was certain that it was my dad. I just knew it 100% in my gut.

I was grateful to the staff. After two weeks, I no longer needed the oxygen. I was well looked after. I appreciate everything they did... but please let me out now! One day, I got myself showered, put some make-up on and dressed myself. I even put my boots on and walked around the ward waiting to prove to the doctor that I was ready to go home. I was so fed up with them taking my blood samples. I had no blood left! Stop testing me! Let me out!

It worked and I was on my way home. Alleluia! Oh, how happy I was! I will never ever take my breath for granted ever again! Breathe. Always remember to breathe because the day you take your last breath is the day you die. Thank God (and my dad) that I was breathing again.

I realised that my ability to recover was strong. I was healthy, my immunity was good, I was resilient and I most importantly I had a positive mind. My defence system was healthy. I was home again. Even today in the Covid pandemic, I feel strong. I have faith in my immune system and my health.

★★★★

I didn't re-start my Garuda classes until much later the following year. I found a tiny but affordable space for four clients maximum close to where I lived. I loved teaching and I was happy again. My classes were flourishing but space was limited. When I found a bigger space in a business centre in Monaco, it was fabulous, and my classes really started to thrive. I had created a warm community of women who loved my classes and we supported each other. I wasn't making a lot of money, but I was able to cover my expenses and I enjoyed our community spirit. Then Covid lockdown hit us in March 2020, putting a brutal stop to all of my classes. All of a sudden, everything just stopped.

I took a couple of classes weekly online like all the other thousands of yoga/Pilates teachers. A few of my clients followed but most of them stopped. Things were so uncertain; it was a difficult time for everyone, and no one wanted to commit to anything. I wasn't entitled to any financial government help as my business was too young and I wasn't making enough money. I was up against a brick wall again. I continued as I could but doing classes a couple of times a week wasn't good for me and it started to take a toll on my body. I was feeling tired, and my body was aching.

I continued my nutrition coaching online. What I loved most about my work as a nutrition and lifestyle coach was bringing out the best in my clients. Yes, I helped them change their relationship with food and yes, they released weight, but so often it wasn't just about the food but about their life. When one client changed their body, they got so much confidence back, they found their soulmate and got married! I was over the moon. When clients started to become aware of any root causes and started to follow their dreams, it made all my coaching seem worthwhile. I valued each individual and wanted to get the best for them whether this be in body, mind or spirit. It was often all three. I empowered them to make better choices.

By the third Covid crisis, and just before summer began, I knew with all the social security contributions in Monaco coming in, that I just wasn't going to financially survive this pandemic, so I called it a day and sadly closed my business in Monaco.

9. My Life Vision
Fifty-Seven to Sixty-Three

I grew up thinking that money was the root of all evil, but I know better now. Money gives you freedom to choose what you do with your time. I never thought about how to make money, which is probably why I have always been broke, but looking back I wish that I had known its value in a more positive way rather than thinking of it as evil.

I could have built a strategy for earning a good income, managing my assets and saving up for the future. I never thought this way; I always lived in the present. What was important was how I felt in the present moment. I would forgive and forget easily and move on. I never bore a grudge with anyone; I had better things to do. I kept moving forward. My vision was so clear, and I could make it happen. Nothing or nobody would stop me once my mind was decided. I always had conviction. I always listened to my heart. I take responsibility for my actions and make the best out of every situation. I am a fighter and I work well under pressure. If I had a deadline, I would always make it no matter what. When I focused, I could do heaps of work.

I could work for an entire day without noticing the time pass. I would always accomplish my goals.

★★★★

Eric and I have been happily married for nine years. When I announced to my parents that I was going to remarry, I heard my mum gasp and say, 'No, are you sure about it?' And my dad quietened her up saying this could be the best thing that could happen to me. At our wedding reception, my dad said how pleased he was that we have both got a second chance of happiness. I realised how true that was. It's okay to not get everything perfect the first time around.

I wish schools taught you the real skills you need in life. I often think of how I would create a whole new system for self-development, lifestyle skills, digging deep to discover who you are and how you will not only survive life but get the most out of it. Why didn't we study real life skills, rather than academic subjects, which I never enjoyed?

With the third Covid lockdown, we moved to our dream house in Provence. We feel safer and Eric can work from home. Technology is amazing and, like many people, we reinvented our ways of working.

★★★★

I have lived in France for thirty years now. I speak fluent French but, even so, it is still not always easy. If you decide to move to France, you will always be a foreigner.

In the beginning it's exciting, but now I am getting tired of it. It takes effort, relationships are challenging, and the culture and humour are very different. You have to relearn everything.

I've always called France home, but due to Covid restrictions I haven't seen my mum or sister for twenty-four months now and I am definitely feeling homesick.

My life belongs here in beautiful Provence but, for the first time ever, I am missing my roots. Feeling homesick is also what encouraged me to write my life story. The funny thing is that, after thirty years, I go home and feel like a foreigner there too, so I find myself having an identity crisis, which is challenging. If you work in France, of course, it's better, but I am no longer working and socialising and it's easy to lose self-confidence.

My advice if you're moving to France is to jump in the deep end. Plunge into the French way of life, mix with the locals. Learn the language and think like a French person. The quicker you settle into a French lifestyle, the easier it will be. Making friends is a tricky one; it can take years and years. Create your own social circle, join communities, get married, have kids and remember to live your life on your terms.

Admin is a nightmare in France, be prepared for ignorant, rude French people. When you meet friendly, kind people count your blessings and give time and attention back to them.

I got lost and I lost my confidence, but eventually I understood why; afterall, I was living overseas, in a foreign country, in a different culture and in two houses, one in the city and one in the countryside. I felt like I missed out on things happening either during the week or at the weekend because I was always in the wrong house. I wasn't working and I lacked social interaction and my self-esteem was low.

I was ready to rebuild myself up again. To reconnect with my roots. I had to stop spreading myself thinly trying to please everyone. What did I really want?

Don't lose yourself, stick to your guns, appreciate what France has to offer you but always remember where you have come from and what your values are.

Airport goodbyes never get any easier and feeling homesick is also part of the package.

I have been very happy here; life is what you make it, just be prepared for a roller coaster journey along the way.

★★★★

One of the greatest things that I have done is to create my life vision. I recommend this to everyone. Take a close look at every category of your life, where you are now and where you would like to be. Having a North Star is something we all need. You have to plan for happiness.

Today my life is devoted to living a healthy lifestyle. I realise that if we don't have our health, we have nothing. We are such a tiny miracle of life. It doesn't take much to be out of balance. Life is such a fragile thing but so resilient too. Like a tiny baby, fragile but strong at the same time.

I am so grateful to be alive. I almost died not once but

twice, yet I am still here. I have changed the direction of my life several times but always landed on my feet. Like a cat with nine lives.

Keep an open mind. Be adaptable and flexible, always ready to bounce back into life. There is so much to do, life is short, and I wasn't going to miss a chance to fulfil my dreams.

Going out on a limb, out of my comfort zone, has always been part of my life and I have never regretted it. I have learnt lessons from each of my life experiences and I really believe that the best is still to come.

I am looking forward to growing older gracefully and enjoying my grandchildren. I am surrounded by love, living in the house of my dreams in the middle of a forest with my husband and my two dogs.

Think about what you truly want out of life, create your own life vision and make it happen. Never give up. Life is not meant to be easy, it's a journey and it will be challenging. Never settle for second best when you can follow your dreams and create the life you choose. You are worth it. You are enough. Create your own happiness. All good things come if you stay focused and never lose sight of what it is your heart desires.

Some people may not understand my life, but that's okay, it's my life. For me, everything has always been connected. I see my vision crystal clear; everything I have ever done was for a reason. I have loved, worked and played strong. There has to be a balance. I have felt totally alone and totally loved. My sons will always be the centre of my heart. They are the most precious gifts I have. Their happiness is everything to me. I hope that I have inspired passion into their lives.

I got a second chance and I got lucky. I found a man who adored me and my kids, he is attentive and supportive. He allowed me to strive towards my passion and when the going got tough he supported me. I encourage his passion too. We have built a good life together. We have survived Covid financially, but we are both ready for a change. We want to stay in the countryside. Rural France is just so pretty with every changing season in our garden.

★★★★

I think of my life like a jigsaw puzzle, and I am creating my life vision one piece at a time. I started back in 2015, when I was shaken up by my first medical scare and left my corporate job. It's all coming together nicely now.

We all make mistakes. Some pieces are the wrong fit, so I have to put them away until I find where they belong, but every piece is relevant to my big picture. Sometimes it flows easily and sometimes I have to search. What I know is that I can see my vision; I know that it is there, and I am getting so close.

★★★★

At fifty-seven, I want to retire. I want to sit in my garden and write my book. This is exactly what I am doing now. I consider myself lucky. I have been so busy trying to make everything work out for me online that I was losing myself again. I need to disconnect from my computer and get outdoors again. Back into the sunlight, back to the birds in my garden; when was the last time I really listened to them?

I have spent time and money trying to create a digital business but is this really what I want? Of course, I would love a constant flow of finances coming in, but not if my head is stuck in my computer all day long. Maybe it's because of Covid, but I am sick and tired of being online. One Zoom call after another, spending way too much time on my computer, enough is enough. I have turned the page again.

Connecting with my deeper self is much more important to me. I need to get back to my roots, go and visit my mum, see my kids, go for a long walk with the dogs. Focus on going in rather than reaching out to others. Everyone has their own life going on, they are all busy, what have I got to offer them which they haven't already got? Yes, imposter syndrome strikes again. Questions and more questions, I just need to clear some space in my head, in my life and breathe.

★★★★

It's amazing how we adapt so quickly. I have now been in the Haut Var, Provence, for four months and going back to Monaco was such a bizarre experience. My first step into our apartment struck me. It felt enclosed, compressing and compact. There was too much furniture, not enough space or light. It was like stepping into a cage. Our apartment is not small, 120m², and yet I felt claustrophobic. I knew that in a day I would be used to it again and so I cherished this moment of awareness to put things right and do the best I could. The amount of clearing out I got done in just one day was impressive. I wanted to leave it better than I had found it because my son was still living there. I couldn't wait to get out and return to the countryside.

★★★★

In Fox, where I now call home, I look out of the windows and I see nature, trees, and colours like greens, yellows, blues and white, birds chattering and space. The silence is golden, and I once again realise how lucky I am. I am not a prisoner in my castle, I am free. I am grateful for everything I have.

★★★★

As I was trying to clear space to write my book, I did some pretty heavy spring cleaning. I looked at what was working in my life, the people that I was connecting with and what value I was getting out of my current business. I had been getting overwhelmed, but I hadn't quite realised just how caught up I was with trying to promote my business. Covid was taking its toll, I was fed up with everything online,

Zoom calls and online networking. I missed meeting people in real life; my website had taken up a lot of time to get it looking good and there were never-ending challenges. I had spent a lot of money investing in marketing skills, but I still didn't feel that I was getting it right, how I wanted it.

When I started writing my book it was like a breath of fresh air. I had made some space, but I had no idea just how much I had cleared. Within days, I had decided to stop trying to sell something that nobody seemed to want. I saw the value in my services and products but whatever marketing I was doing wasn't getting people interested enough to buy. I was tired of trying.

It didn't help that my husband's phone never stopped ringing. I realised the meaning of a successful business and I felt like a failure. I decided it was time to focus on myself again. Be the role model, lead, share my journey and get the results I wanted for my clients. Inspire others and let people come to me.

Once my decision was taken, I cancelled everything. I had no money coming in. I closed my website reluctantly because I loved how it looked now but it didn't bring me any clients, so what was the point? I closed my business in Monaco and cancelled monthly subscriptions to numerous sites.

The only thing I kept was The Writing Academy. I felt a breath of fresh air in the Academy and tremendous support from Cassandra Farren and other fellow members. Everyone had a dream to become an author and we were encouraging each other, there was no competition, everyone's story was unique, and I loved this positivity.

★★★★

The French have a certain *je ne sais quoi* for life! I was attracted to France for this reason. I must have been very intuitive from a young age to have sensed this but, after thirty years of living here, I know that this natural lifestyle is what I have always loved. The French know how to enjoy life. They know how to enjoy the very essence of happiness, to love and laugh and spend quality time with family and friends. It is a trait that I have always admired. It has naturally become part of who I am too.

I am not French but not British either and it is often difficult to find the balance between the two. I think this is where my weakness is. The two cultures are so different, the humour is different, and it can feel quite conflicting, like balancing on a small wire trying not to fall off on either side. I assume this is how I lost myself in the first place.

I'm taken back to my greatest joy, a French marketplace. I feel the vibrations of energy; a mix of locals and tourists. It is an exquisite sensory place as I stroll around touching, smelling, feeling, hearing and seeing all the wonders of the marketplace. I love watching the people. Some will take their time and stop to sample local delicacies; it's so thrilling to taste everything. Others will be whipping around picking up what they need before they rush home to prepare their lunch. I personally prefer to wander. Following my nose and eyes and allowing myself to be under the spell of everything that is on offer.

I love the fresh fruit and vegetables best. There is so much choice and freshness, it is thrilling, like a child in a sweet shop. This is my real pleasure in life now as I get older; being able to fill my basket with colourful fresh produce, which I know will keep me healthy. As I walk around the market, I still wonder at so much variety and richness. I can taste the watermelons and mangoes; I can touch the fruits and the different textures of the vegetables. My mind is a whirl as I imagine what I can prepare for lunch and then dinner.

I love the colourful linens and tablecloths of all shapes and sizes. I love choosing a pretty tablecloth and here the choice is unlimited. Then I get to the spices, oh here I feel quite exotic, the smells are enticing, and I get an urge to make a curry or maybe even a couscous.

I don't buy a lot of herbs because they don't keep and, besides, my garden is full of rosemary and thyme and these Provençal herbs are the ones I usually use in my kitchen. I love using what grows locally. If I'm lucky, I will have courgettes in my garden, even melons, green beans, peas and tomatoes. One year we had so much squash we couldn't eat it all, so I froze it and we had it all year. In summer I love the fresh fruits. All the berries, strawberries, raspberries, blueberries and blackberries, it still amazes me that as a kid I didn't like them. How our tastes change as we grow older.

Occasionally there will be a fishmonger and I will buy fresh fish, but where we live it is more of a hunter's ground. There will be fresh meat and poultry and even cooked meats, which are so delicious they can be eaten with a simple fresh crispy green salad from the garden.

There are baskets galore, too many to buy, but I love looking at them. I love their colours and shapes and if you're really lucky you'll see the basket weaver with his clever fingers swiftly weaving his baskets. There is something very French about going to the market with your basket dangling over your arm and I enjoy it so much.

★★★★

I'm distracted! let's come back to my life vision. Was I too young to retire?

In the summer of 2021, my husband and I decided to bring our retirement plan forward and we opened our home to bed and breakfast. I immediately loved hosting our guests. I was happy to have some social interaction and I became alive again. It was intensive at times, there was lots of cleaning and washing, but I loved having a clean house and making up beds with fresh sheets. I enjoyed the morning run to our local boulangerie to buy fresh bread and croissants. I was up early, before anyone, and it felt good to be out and about before our guests woke up.

I loved serving breakfast in our beautiful garden. It truly is paradise. The birds are singing, and I feel alive, connected to my soul again. Life is good.

★★★★

I haven't written for a while. Summer has been busy. From the moment we decided to open our B&B, bookings started to flow in. Our first guests arrived on my birthday, the 2nd of July. We hosted a young couple from Nice and we had such a wonderful evening together with champagne and birthday cake. This is what I have been missing since Covid; real life interactions, social contacts and real conversations.

The money flowed in, much to my delight, and although it was quite intensive, I enjoyed hosting and proposing a variety of breakfast options. We offered a delicious evening meal, which I enjoyed planning for. We would always have an aperitif, then tapenade or a verrine with prawns and avocado. Our main dish would be typically Provençale like stuffed vegetables, fish with aïoli sauce or filet mignon with mushrooms and cream with wine, of course. Sometimes for a change we would make an exotic wok-style dish with cashew nuts and colourful vegetables. Dessert would be a fresh fruit salad or tarte aux pommes. We would open a good bottle of red wine and I would dress up for dinner ready to welcome our guests. We would eat outside once the heat of the day died down and there was occasionally a light welcoming breeze and with muted lighting and candles I loved these long summer evenings.

July and August were intensive. We live in a popular summer location close to Lac St. Croix and the famous canyons les Gorges du Verdon. Throughout the summer, our home was full of guests travelling around France. It made me feel worthy, I had a new purpose in life, and everyone loved it at Crazy Foxy Retreats, as I'd fondly called our new adventure.

By the end of August, we were getting tired. The dogs were a handful – always keeping them well behaved was a challenge in itself – and looking after guests every day that were in and out of the house was tiring. We were glad when September came. We were ready for a rest. We needed to breathe, have our own space and even the dogs needed their own space back again.

****

I have been awake all night gathering my thoughts together and I had to get up to write. It is the 8th of September at 03:54 and I just realised that love has been an integral part of my wanting to come to France in the first place. I was head over heels in love when I arrived and, as a Cancer, I need to surround myself with a loving cocoon in order to flourish… if I feel loved, I can do anything. If I have doubts or lack confidence I am limited. The moments I have felt the most love are the moments that I have flourished the most. I woke up needing to put pen to paper to capture these intense feelings, knowing that I had just identified a pattern throughout my life.

****

Once married for the second time, I had a routine. Eric would leave early before I got up; he would be home at

12:15 on the dot for his lunch and leave at 13:15 before returning at 18:15

My life started to revolve around his routine. I would get up and work till 11:30 then make lunch. We always had a dog, so I would go out with the dogs, but I seemed to lose touch with my girlfriends. I tried to make a conscious effort to reconnect with them, at least those that were worth it, as I have said goodbye to many along my journey.

We are a good couple. We enjoy going out, having a nice meal, socialising and relaxing. Covid has changed things; we are now in the countryside, we have turned inwards, worked in our garden, planted our vegetables, cooked together, shared together and loved together. They are happy days.

Whatever I was trying to be has less importance now. I don't have anything to prove to anyone but myself. I need to just look after myself and my family.

****

My mum has always been my role model. She is pretty, slim and strong. She has character and patience. She was always the peacekeeper in our family. I still look up to her. Now at over eighty, Mum can still climb a mountain, rear chickens and carry a bale of hay to the horses. I remember when I was a kid; I entered a competition for Mother's Day. I had to complete the phrase: 'My mum is the best mum in the world because…' and I wrote, '…she can toss pancakes'. It was published in the local newspaper, and I was so proud of her.

She used to spend hours sewing my costumes for the numerous dance festivals that I attended, she was a talented dressmaker – she could make anything – and she always worked. She used to have lodgers and make a full English breakfast every morning before everyone left for work or, in my case, school. The smell was heavenly and enough to get anyone out of bed.

Mum was also a talented secretary. She did shorthand, admin, accounts and PA work. She was the best. When Dad worked abroad, she would do temporary contracts in between her travels, and they always wanted to keep her. When I was at high school, my mum was the school secretary and I loved knowing that she was never far away.

★★★★

Dad was a giver. If you were in need, he would be there. He looked out for his own mum until he died, and Ruby Nana is still alive to this day at 103 years old. When I broke my arm, he was on the first plane and drove me everywhere for the next three months. I feel like I missed some episodes in my dad's life. When he had a heart bypass while I was dancing my heart out in Paris, I never realised what was going on. I regretted afterwards that I had not been there. We didn't always see eye to eye, but I admired him. He taught me passion and determination, and to follow my dreams.

Being overseas, we had a better understanding of each other, and he would always be there to pick up the phone. When he died suddenly, I was in shock. How was it possible? Not my dad… it was a very painful time, I thought I would never smile or laugh again. But, of course, I did, and time does heal. It still hurts so much that I wasn't there when he died suddenly.

★★★★

It's funny but throughout my life dance has always brought me back on track. It always brings me home. I can be out of my comfort zone anywhere but put me in a dance class anywhere in the world and I will feel at home. Maybe it's because I was good at it. I felt comfortable, at ease, confident, happy, and connected. I started dancing, after all, when I was just four years old. I can look at old photos and now from my experienced eye I can see that my talent was just waiting for the right time to blossom.

★★★★

Clearing space has been such a valid practice to refocus my mind and get some clarity into my life. Whether it's clearing a cupboard, sorting out my wardrobe or cutting down shrubs and trees in my garden, I am on a surge. The space that I am creating is wonderful. I can see the light pouring in. I feel like I am cleansing myself. I'm used to a food detox, but this is different, I feel like I am allowing myself space to breathe, to renew my energy. I have let go of social media contacts, emails, website subscriptions, training courses, ecommerce and technical challenges. I have stopped it all. I am reconnecting with myself.

I am getting out into nature, allowing myself time, allowing the warmth of the sun to soak into my body, to re-energise myself, to breathe deeply. I need to let go of my anxiety. I realise that I am actually exactly where I am supposed to be right now. I am enough.

I have released the weight of expectations from my shoulders. I am ME again. I feel free. I feel happy again. I am flowing in the space around me. Like a dance, like a vibration or the movement of a wave. Nothing can stop me. I am reconnecting with my inner self, and it feels so good.

★★★★

September came and I asked myself what I would do now.

So, I've started to attend a local jazz class, not as a teacher, but for my own pleasure. It is a Matt Mattox advanced jazz class, which is challenging me to get my aching body moving again. It is thrilling to be in a dance studio again, just like always, and I immediately loved it.

I don't have to be perfect; I just have to work with the best version of me today. This is my new mantra (thanks Ariel).

I am also back on track with mindful eating again (thanks WILDFIT®). No more aperitifs, bread or ice cream; no, I must lose some more weight if I want to age gracefully like my mum. This is once again my priority, so let's see how I get on over the next few weeks.

★★★★

It's amazing how, as soon as I connect again with dance, I feel a buzz. I have always said that throughout my life, through the ups and downs, dance has always been my constant that has brought me back on track. I'm not sure if it's the discipline or just the excitement of being in a dance studio again. I feel alive. It is also helping me to feel younger and fit again. The more I move my body, the more I love it. I am so lucky to have found a Matt Mattox jazz class so close to my village and an advanced class! I feel suddenly alive again and I love feeling like anything is possible. I know that it will help raise my self-confidence again and surely it can only be good for my body.

I have reframed my mind. I don't have to be perfect. I am fifty-seven. I am allowed to be just as I am. I can just do my best and make progress. When I was younger, of course I could do it all, but every one of us could say that, right? So now I just want to feel happiness dancing. I don't even want to be teaching, I just want to enjoy my class. It really is a luxury, a gift that I can give myself. I know that this new jazz class is good for me. It feels like returning to my world of magic.

I feel the usual thrill that dance gives me, and I know in my gut that this is the right decision. It gets me out meeting people again, socially interacting and that is wonderful too. I sat in the jacuzzi massaging my aching feet thinking how lucky I am. It's a beautiful day.

★★★★

I hate this Covid virus. It's not doing anyone any good. Social distancing indeed! We are humans, socially interacting and communicating with each other is what makes us human. Stop taking that away from us. We all need to fight to keep our freedom. Listen to your instincts my friends, listen to your heart.

★★★★

Here I go again, "doubting Thomas", asking myself if I am good enough, thinking I am too old, wanting to give up on myself. Feeling guilty for going and guilty for not going. Let me explain. My jazz class makes me feel alive, takes me back to the old ME and I love the studio space and the atmosphere. It makes me feel like me again and I feel good. But recently I have been feeling tired, old and doubting myself again.

Today I went to class early to say I wasn't coming during the winter months, knowing that if I stopped now that would be it, I couldn't pick it up again and I so wanted to do better. I just didn't think I had the energy…

Angie was amazing. She sat me down and really listened to me then told me all the reasons why she didn't want to lose me and how I would always be a dancer. She said I was her best meeting of the year and that she was telling everyone about me! Imagine that!

She understood what I was going through and reassured

me that it was all normal and that sitting at home wasn't going to make it better, and yes, she's right. She said that I was part of a family now and that we had so much to share together and, of course, her kind words touched my heart, and I broke down. She told me that I had the sensibility of a true artist and that I would always be a dancer. At last, here was someone who really understood me with all my fears, my doubts and my apprehensions. She shared so much love that I realised I couldn't give up. So, I would be back in the studio the following week. Thank you, Angie, for holding me up when I felt like I was falling and giving up on myself again. Back in the studio, I was dancing and loving every moment… as I knew I would. Life is about lifting ourselves up, loving ourselves enough to keep going.

★★★★

On 1st of November, I'll have known Eric for eleven years. I can't believe how time has flown by. As I look back over these years, I realise how much we have achieved together. We have created a new life for ourselves.

Now that my sons are adults, they get on so much better and they fill me with pride. My love for them is unconditional. A mother's love can never be replaced. I will always be here for them no matter what happens. I am so proud of them. Julien is now a valued crew member of British Airways travelling all over the world, and also International Community Manager for an internet game I will never understand. He has a chic flat in London but who knows where life will take him in the future. He is loyal to his friends and family, and I miss him a lot.

David is still in Monaco. He has made excellent progress as a bilingual accountant, and he is a well valued and popular team member who also still finds time to excel in trail running. He has always shown support and kindness and I wish him the very best in life because he deserves the best. I watch him falling in love and I am the happiest mum in the world. It is my greatest role in life; then, now and forever.

As I read through my book, I realise how much my life has been constantly evolving. Circumstances I have controlled, decisions I have made, as well as others beyond my control like the pandemic, have created change. It is all okay, we are living human beings, we are emotional creatures, we are supposed to have emotions. This is how I like life, emotional, flowing like a dance. My life dance. I don't need to know what tomorrow will bring because I know that I will adapt. I know that I have the resources to make the most out of any situation. I am responsible for my happiness.

Between my first breath and my last breath everything in between belongs to me, it's my life. Dare to dream big, my friends, follow your instincts, follow your passion, live every moment in the present, love and happiness are what life is all about.

10. To Be Revealed
Sixty-Four to Seventy...

Epiphany.

My grandmother passed away peacefully in her sleep. She was 103 years and 8 months. People often asked her, 'What is your remedy for long life?' Her answer was always laughter. She vowed by smashed banana on toast with honey for breakfast and she always had a twinkle in her eye. Ruby Nana we will miss you. I am left feeling sad and sorry. Sorry that I can't get to the funeral to be with my family at this time. We are now in the fifth wave of Covid-19. I would need at least six covid tests to be able to fly to the UK and be released out of quarantine to attend the funeral. It is times like this when I feel alone and homesick and that I should be with my family across the seas. It is always hard and never gets any easier. I am scared that I will never be able to leave France again with the Covid travel restrictions in place. My heart is torn between staying safe and leaving. My mind tells me one thing and my heart tells me another. Usually, I follow my heart, but this situation is beyond my control, and I feel helpless. One day, when all of this pandemic is behind us, we will have a huge party and our whole family can get together to celebrate life again.

This is what you will have to accept if you come and live in France, that you will often feel alone and always far away from loved ones back home. There are times that you just wish that you could transport yourself back to your roots. Family will always be family and there is a price to pay for everything. Follow your dreams but make sure that it is what you really want and be prepared to make sacrifices along the way. Happiness only comes if you accept yourself and love yourself wholeheartedly.

A successful life can be counted by how many happy days you live and love. Ruby Nana was right, it is laughter that keeps you young, so keep smiling, my friend, always look on the bright side and keep laughing. Life is a dance, just keep flowing.

Bonus: My Seven Steps to Heaven

Are you thinking of moving to France?

Here are what I like to call my seven steps to heaven:

1. Make connections. Do this as soon as you move to France and start settling in. Join associations and get yourself out and about. Mix with the locals. You never know who you may meet.

2. Learn French. Practice as much as you can. Make mistakes and learn from them. Always try your best to speak the language whenever you can. Make French friends.

3. Visualise what it is you want. Get clarity in all areas of your life. Dream big and start building your vision. Start small, one step at a time, each day do something towards creating the life you choose.

4. Educate yourself. Retrain if you need to. Get a job. Remember the talents you already have. Believe in yourself. You are good enough. You are unique.

5. Create self-care habits. Remember who you are and look after yourself. Remember the importance of breathing. Surround yourself with positive friends.

6. Respect your own values and beliefs. Don't lose yourself. Let go of any limiting beliefs and focus on what you have already achieved. Always appreciate the present moment.

7. Keep track of your challenges and how you make progress. Stay organised. Use what motivates you and lead with your actions. Inspire others and celebrate every success. Make life fun, always look for a positive side and keep smiling.

Acknowledgements

Thank you to my sons Julien and David for giving me so much joy in life. I am so proud of the kind, handsome young men that you have grown into. Believe in yourselves, dream big, open your wings and fly high, my darlings, you can achieve anything you desire. You are so worthy and deserve the very best. I love you.

Thank you to my husband Eric for giving us both a second chance at love and happiness. You have always been here for me and without you I couldn't have achieved all that I have done. Loving you has made me a very happy woman and I thank you from the bottom of my heart.

Thank you to my friends, in real life and online. To Samantha, Melanie, Fabienne and Vilde who have always been there for me. So many online friends too, you will never realise how important you have been in my life, cheering me on and picking me up when I was low, I hope that one day our paths will cross.

Thank you to my Garuda community of friends who gave me so much love and hope for better things to come before Covid-19 put an abrupt stop to our classes. I miss you all.

Thank you to all my nutrition clients with whom I

have coached and shared my wellness journey. In touching your lives, you too have touched mine and I am grateful.

Thank you to everyone who has helped make this book a reality, and especially my beautiful and inspirational book mentor, Cassandra Farren from Welford Publishing. Thank you for your guidance.

Thank you to the wonderful Jen from Fuzzy Flamingo for your insights and creativity in designing my book and making it all happen.

Thank you to my teachers and mentors, my original dance teachers; Miss Gale and Miss Anne, Michelle Scott, Joan Darwall, Jacqueline Ferguson and Phrosso Pfister.

I acknowledge Colin Field who opened professional doors for me, George Geddes and Leila Mikail. I would also like to thank Eric Edmeades and Jon and Missy for changing my life with your thought-provoking philosophies. I am grateful that they opened my mind to endless possibilities.

Thank you to all my four-legged soulmates, Hobo, Tobi, my beloved Max, George, Buddy and Ruby; what would I have done without you? I love you all.

And last but not least, thank you to my mum, dad and sister Kat, you are my family, I would never have got this far without your support, I love you.

"Families are like branches of a tree.
We grow in different directions,
yet our roots remain as one"

~ Unknown

About the author

Lisa lives in Provence with her husband Eric and their two dogs Ruby and Buddy. Lisa promotes a healthy lifestyle and encourages others to follow their dreams. She grows her own vegetables and loves to create healthy meals. Her passion for dance is still part of her life and her readers are welcome to visit at Crazy Foxy Retreats (B&B) which brings her a lot of joy and happiness. Lisa is looking forward to growing old gracefully, becoming a grandmother and still being in love at 100 years old!

Contact me:

I would love to hear from you!

Please send your feedback, a review, ask any questions you may have or just follow my adventures.

Email: Lifepassion98000@gmail.com

Facebook: https://www.facebook.com/LGT06

Instagram: https://www.instagram.com/livinginprovence/

Printed in Great Britain
by Amazon